T0068981

DEFENCE OF HOUSES

By
COLONEL G. A. WADE, M.C.

AUTHOR OF
" The Defence of Bloodford Village," etc.

ALDERSHOT :
GALE & POLDEN LIMITED
Price One Shilling and Sixpence net
(By post 1/8)

PLATE 1

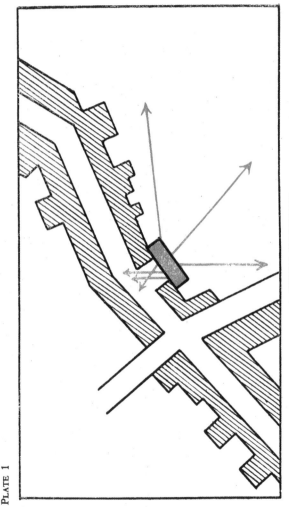

A GOOD POSITION

Usually a house which is set back from the general building line is a good one to defend.

An enemy coming along the street cannot fire at the defenders and is caught in sudden concentrated fire as shown.

Incidentally, the fact that the building is set back enables it to enfilade the rear of other buildings in the street—a very useful point.

SUMMARY

WHEN INVASION COMES.
>Most stubborn fighting in **built-up areas.**
>Houses—infinite variety.
>Tanks hate houses.

CHOICE OF HOUSE TO DEFEND.
>Tactical considerations.
>Relation to general defence scheme.
>Is it **strong**?—Machine-gun fire.
>" Jerry " builders.
>Has it a **cellar**?
>Are surroundings suitable?
>Field of fire—50 or 100 yards.
>Inconspicuousness.
>Means of approach.
>Dominating points.
>Trenches in garden.
>End houses—place in **row.**
>Set-back buildings (Plate 1).

MUTUAL SUPPORT.
>Co-operation of defended houses (Plate 2).
>Three supporting worth twelve independent.

ALL-ROUND DEFENCE.
>Consider from enemy's point of view.
>**Every direction at all times.**

IMPROVEMENTS.
>Engineering work.

LOOPHOLES.
>Ample number—move after firing.
>Best near ground.
>Corner loopholes (Plate 3).
>Unexpected places (Plate 4).
>Below eaves or windows (Plate 5).
>Keep muzzle out of sight (Plate 6).
>Never use **enemy**-made loopholes.
>Netting, to stop grenades (Plate 7).
>Danger of light (Plate 8).
>Bullet-proofing.
>Half-filled sandbag as rifle rest.
>**Dummies** in loopholes.
>Sandbags to catch bullets.

3

PLATE 2

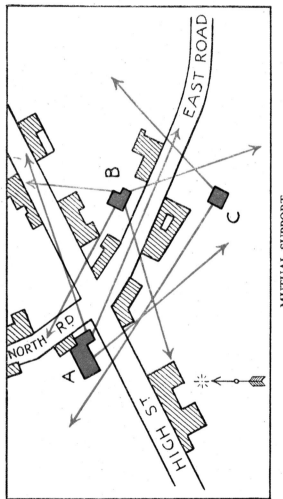

MUTUAL SUPPORT

These three buildings are so sited as to be a source of strength to one another.

The arrows indicate how each house, stoutly held, will deny to the enemy covered approaches to the other two.

In such circumstances the three houses TOGETHER represent much more opposition to the enemy's advance than three independent houses.

Emission of smoke or light.
Throwing grenades out.
Flaps in wire netting.
14-inch wall in three minutes.
Mirrors at loopholes.
Camouflage (Plate 9).
Checker pattern loopholes through **inside walls**
(Plate 10).
Loopholes through ceilings (Plate 11).
Loopholes through floors (Plate 12).
Bayonet loopholes (Plate 13).
" Up the grating " (Plate 14).
Loopholed traverse (Plate 15).
Site firing position **well back** (Plate 16).
Obvious loopholes to deter enemy.
Twenty-six points have been mentioned.
" You will discover twenty-six more."

SHORING UP.

Need for supporting floor (Plate 17).
Two exits necessary.

WINDOWS AND DOORS.

Blocking with shingle.

THE ROOF.

Can enemy get on roof?
Put snipers on flat roofs.
Communications—visual or speaking-tube.

ENTRANCES.

Barricade or protect by loopholed traverse.
Make entries into traps.
Inter-communication—**cellars.**
Passages room to room.
Screens.

UPWARD FIRE.

Arrange protection for men upstairs.

SANITARY ARRANGEMENTS.

H.E. world's finest laxative.

GAS-PROOF A ROOM.

Preferably the strengthened one.

OUTSIDE.

Clear the field of fire cunningly.
Make cover a **death-trap.**

PLATE 3

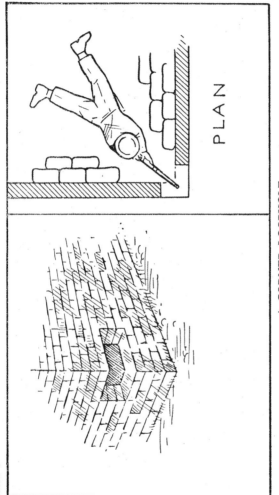

PLAN

A CORNER LOOPHOLE

Frequently the corner of a building affords an unusually good field of fire. In the illustration the loophole is very obvious. Actually it would be camouflaged in some way, such as two bushes in front of it with space to fire under or between them; or a large piece of ivy can be transplanted from a neighbouring house to climb over it.

Note the rifleman is well protected by sandbags.

Dummy cover to influence line of attack.
Outhouses and garages.
Fire **through** buildings.
Make **vulnerable** areas low down.

BARBED WIRE.
Must **not** be seen by enemy.
Coils in entries, alleys, passages.
Hang tins on wire.
Must be **covered by fire.**

DOMINATING POSITIONS.
Look for them.
Occupy them or cover with fire.

DEAD GROUND.
Detached post may be needed.

APPROACHES.
Day and night for rations, etc.

NO INDICATION TO ENEMY.
Treat neighbouring houses in same way.

ATTACK IS THE BEST DEFENCE.
Prepare for **counter-attacks.**

FIRE.
Remove inflammable refuse.
Collect equipment.
Water and sand.
Cut off gas and electricity.

THE MEN.
Get **right idea** about what men will do.
Dismiss lingering **Maginot** complex.
Not a place to await the enemy !
House centre for activity in surrounding areas.
" Dart out and sting! "
May be last desperate stand.
Only a few men required.
To act as garrison, cooks, etc.
House used for feeding and rest.
Fighting patrols come and go.
Concerned now with **garrison only.**
Organized in pairs.
Constant look-out.
Reserve for emergency.

PLATE 4

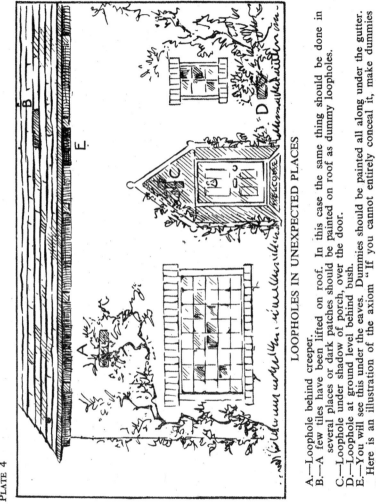

LOOPHOLES IN UNEXPECTED PLACES

A.—Loophole behind creeper.
B.—A few tiles have been lifted on roof. In this case the same thing should be done in several places or dark patches should be painted on roof as dummy loopholes.
C.—Loophole under shadow of porch, over the door.
D.—Loophole at ground level behind bush.
E.—You will see this under the eaves. Dummies should be painted all along under the gutter. Here is an illustration of the axiom "If you cannot entirely conceal it, make dummies like it."

AUTOMATIC WEAPONS.
Wiser to put where **poor field of fire.**

BOMBS AND MINES.
Prepare for action.

SNIPERS.
Posted in surrounding district.
Withdrawal instructions.

LIAISON.

CORRECT TACTICS.
The Mairie (Plate 18).
Narrate the action.
Errors.

(1) **Assumed** enemy would attack from SOUTH. Had not sent out **scouts** or kept **all-round watch.**

(2) Placed automatic weapons where he **hoped** enemy would come.

(3) Not occupied the **roof.**

(4) Put **barbed wire** in wrong place.

(5) Not barricaded **doors.**

(6) Not protected **stairs.**

(7) Wasted time.

(8) Not kept reserve.

We must do **best we can** with **material available.**

LET YOUR DEFENCE BE ACTIVE—GO OUT AND **HIT THE ENEMY FIRST**—KEEP ON HITTING HIM.

Have your DEFENCE SO GOOD AND SO CUNNING that when enemy is about to attack you can say:

" And NOW HE'S GOING TO ASK FOR IT AND HE WILL **GET IT** ! "

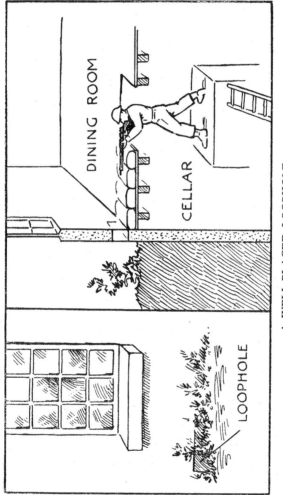

PLATE 5

A WELL-PLACED LOOPHOLE

On the left you see the loophole cunningly concealed by the flowers in the border. On the right is a section of the house showing the dining-room and the cellar below. The floor has been cut away to enable the rifleman to pop up from the cellar and fire.

You will observe that the man is practically below ground when firing, but even the small part of him which is exposed has been protected by FOUR sandbags!

Attention to details like this will cut down the casualty list.

DEFENCE OF HOUSES

THIS is a very important subject and one which well repays a little earnest study.

When the enemy invade us the most stubborn fighting will be in the built-up areas where their tanks will not be able to help them much, and if in these places the houses have been scientifically prepared for defence it may make all the difference to the result, and in any case will have considerable influence upon the casualties suffered by the defending forces.

Houses are found in infinite variety. Some are very suited for defence, others are absolute death-traps.

Frequently the tactical situation will demand that a certain house, or houses, will have to be held regardless of suitability. In this case we have to improve them as much as possible with the means at our disposal.

Sometimes, however, we may be able to choose which house or houses we intend to defend, and when we have a choice the following are the chief considerations which should influence us in making our decision.

THE TACTICAL SITUATION

Is the house where, if held, it will best assist the general defence scheme?

Possibly the intention is to defend a road block or an important road junction, and in this case a house must be chosen which is placed so that adequate fire can be brought to bear upon the tactical point.

It may be that several houses are equally good from this standpoint, so the one should be chosen which is best in the following respects: —

(1) Is it Strong ?

Houses vary tremendously, and when assessing the strength of the building remember that close-range machine-gun fire is very penetrative, as a number of bullets will hit exactly the same brick.

PLATE 6

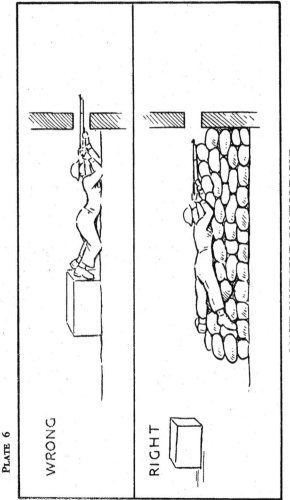

WRONG

RIGHT

MAKE YOURSELF COMFORTABLE

The top man is too idle to move the box, so he has to push his muzzle right out into the enemy's view. All we can do with that type of man is to hope his end will be painless.

The lower man is well back from the loophole, has arranged sandbags to rest his rifle on and protect him in front. Not only that; as he is upstairs he has taken precautions against upward fire from below.

Each successive bullet starts penetrating where the previous one left off and a long burst will consequently eat its way through quite a lot of masonry. The house may be subjected to aerial bombing, trench-mortaring, or artillery fire, consequently the stronger it is the better.

Usually, the newer the house the less robust it is; in fact, most of the modern houses surrounding our towns seem to have been erected by the Fifth Column specially to act as traps for the defenders.

From this standpoint, the expression " Jerry builder " has acquired a new and sinister significance!

(2) Has it a Cellar ?

A cellar is very desirable. It can be made safe and is where stores, ammunition, water, candles, etc., can be stored and where wounded may be kept pending evacuation.

(3) Are its Surroundings Suitable ?

The house will be a difficult proposition to defend if there are covered approaches to it on several sides and no reasonable field of fire.

By "reasonable field of fire" I do not mean several hundred yards. In some circumstances 50 or 100 yards will be as good as you can hope for.

If the building to be defended harmonizes with its surroundings and is not conspicuous, so much the better.

Another factor in the surroundings is the means of approach, and departure. Where it is possible to move into and out of the house under cover from enemy observation this might be an enormous advantage to the defence.

You must also carefully study the surroundings to see if there is any dominating point such as a neighbouring high building or hill from which the enemy could bring close-range fire to bear.

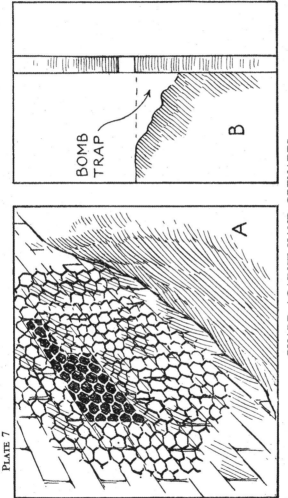

PLATE 7

GUARD AGAINST HAND GRENADES

There is always wire netting available near houses and some of this should be firmly nailed round loopholes, particularly the low ones.

If the loophole is actually at ground level a trench for the grenade to explode in after it has rolled off the netting should be arranged as shown on the right.

Unless you do this, fragments of the grenade may enter the loophole.

A garden in which trenches could be dug for protection against bombing is always an asset.

Frequently a splendid place to select is a house in a ROW! Do not select end houses if you can help it, as they are so liable to be punished by the enemy's mortars and machine guns. If only one or two houses in a row are occupied the enemy has to find out *which* they are and that will cost him casualties. A building which is set back from the other buildings in the row frequently offers advantages for defence (Plate 1).

(4) Is it where it can be Supported ?

There may be other defended houses in the locality and mutual protection might be arranged from one house, but not from another. This is a most important point (Plate 2).

Three or four defended houses sited so as to be mutually supporting are worth a dozen houses defended independently.

(5) Is it Capable of All-round Defence ?

When you have decided which house or houses you will hold you should first of all consider them from the enemy's point of view and imagine from which direction he will attack and what tactics he will use. This will influence you in deciding where you will arrange your loopholes, your wire, your booby traps, your alarms, and your general welcome for the strangers.

Remember above all things that the house must be capable of being defended from EVERY DIRECTION AT ALL TIMES.

If it is in the centre of a row, loopholes should be put through the walls into the houses on either side.

Well, having duly considered all these points and decided on which house you will defend and from which direction attack will most probably come, we now have to begin improving it by all kinds of engineering work. First of all, let us arrange

15

PLATE 8

A FATAL ERROR

A simple sketch, but a tragic one. It shows how hundreds of good men have brought about their own deaths.

It may be light from another loophole, it may be from the door, or a candle, or EVEN A CIGARETTE!

The enemy sniper, waiting patiently, sees the head silhouetted in the loophole, aligns his sight and squeezes the trigger.

A blanket hung *behind* the look-out's head would have prevented this tragedy.

THE LOOPHOLES

There should be an ample number of loopholes so that when a man has fired from one, and thereby possibly given away his position, he can move to another one before the enemy takes retaliatory action. The most effective loopholes are usually those nearest to the ground. A loophole in the corner of the building is strong and useful (Plate 3).

Try to get loopholes in *unexpected places* (Plate 4), such as under the overhanging eaves, just below windows, at ground level and so on (Plate 5). See that it is possible for a rifleman to get his muzzle well back from the loophole (Plate 6). Many a good man has gone west because an enemy sniper using glasses or telescopic sights has picked up the dull glint of his protruding muzzle.

Incidentally, if ever you capture a house from the enemy NEVER USE THE ENEMY'S LOOPHOLES; if you do, you will be asking for it.

Loopholes, particularly those which are low down, should be fixed up with a wire-netting cover to stop grenades (Plate 7). Take every care to ensure that no light of any kind shows through the loophole to an observer outside, otherwise a man will have his head silhouetted when he mans the loophole and he will not last long (Plate 8).

All around the loophole should be made absolutely bullet-proof with sandbags or steel plate, and in each one should be placed a half-filled sandbag for the rifleman to rest his weapon on.

An excellent ruse is to have a few dummies with strings attached which can be made to move so as to be JUST FAINTLY VISIBLE in a loophole. And this reminds me to warn you about something—every loophole is a source of danger to those in the house because at any moment a bullet may come flying through it into the room. You should therefore be sure that sandbags filled with shingle are arranged behind each loophole to prevent this.

PLATE 9

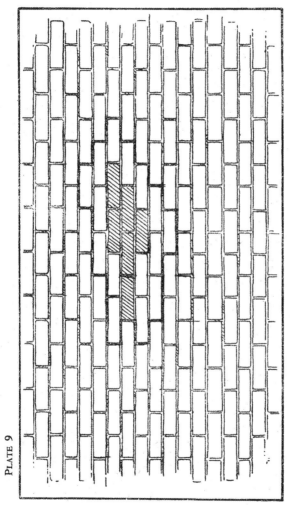

TO CAMOUFLAGE A LOOPHOLE

Knock out the loophole, irregular in shape. Nail open canvas, gauze or perforated zinc over it as shown. Trim so that edge of camouflage material comes on the joints between bricks and then paint to match the bricks and mortar.

You will be astonished how transparent this is from *inside* and how difficult to detect from outside. If you have great difficulty in matching the walls exactly try painting the wall to match the camouflage.

Take precautions to prevent smoke by day and light by night from issuing from the loopholes. This is a point easily overlooked and it may tell the enemy everything he wants to know.

All loopholes should be so arranged that a grenade can be thrown OUT through them; if necessary a flap should be left in any wire netting put over them.

With a crowbar and sledge-hammer it is possible to loophole a 14-inch wall in three minutes, so do not be mean with them. It is good to have plenty, provided, of course, that they are not obvious to the enemy.

If the house happens to be a furnished one you may be able to fix one or two mirrors at loopholes so that a man can sit in safety and watch what is happening outside. When you do this, be sure it is *dark* inside the room and that the mirrors cannot move so as to reflect the light from outside.

Loopholes can be camouflaged in lots of ways, one of the best being to cover the loophole with perforated zinc of the kind used to keep flies out of meat stores, or with gauze or wide-mesh canvas, and get somebody with artistic ability to paint it like the surrounding bricks and mortar. Perfectly astounding results can be obtained in this way, it being impossible to detect the loophole at twenty yards' distance and yet from inside the room (which MUST be kept dark) a perfectly clear view of the enemy can be obtained (Plate 9).

Where it is difficult to hide the loopholes, a checker pattern painted all over, like the old-fashioned forts, will help considerably.

So far we have talked only about loopholes through the outside walls of buildings, but a few loopholes actually inside the house to enable fire to be brought to bear from one room into another will help tremendously should the Germans succeed in forcing an entry (Plate 10). Loopholes through floors also have their uses, either for firing down into the room below (Plate 11) or up into the room above (Plate 12).

A bayonet loophole at the side of a passage may be invaluable. If an enemy comes along the passage he

PLATE 10

LOOPHOLE THE INSIDE WALLS

In the above case a loophole has been knocked through the wall between two rooms, and the table has been placed to hide it. The wall is shown cut away in the drawing so that you can see the man who has just bagged a "right and left" with buck-shot from a 12-bore.

Incidentally, if the invader on the left could see the expression on the hidden defender's face as he reloads he would not stand with his hands up. He would be through the door like a rabbit!

can be disposed of *without a sound*. The bayonet loop-hole should be small and about 3 ft 6 in. from the ground to enable the enemy to be struck in the kidneys just after he has passed (Plate 13).

Sometimes there are gratings in pavements and passages which can be used as loopholes for upward shots (Plate 14).

Incidentally, never, if you can help it, fire over the top of a wall where your head will be very obvious. A loophole low down is much safer.

A terrible obstacle in house-to-house fighting is a loopholed traverse (Plate 15). If it is well sited and strongly made, it is exceedingly difficult to pass when a determined man is behind it.

If you are siting a loophole where the enemy may occupy some place either above or below and fire into it from close to, be sure to site the firing position *well* back (Plate 16).

Should there be one side of the house where your defences are weak and you are anxious that the enemy should not choose it for his attack, make a few moderately obvious loopholes there. The sight of these may induce him to attack one of the other sides, which will suit you a lot better.

That covers loopholes. As a matter of fact, they are very interesting things, and I have just mentioned twenty-six points in connection with them. When you come to study them you will discover twenty-six more.

Next let us consider strengthening the cellar or a downstairs room, remembering always that if you are going to put considerable weight on to a floor by sand-bagging, etc., you must support it adequately underneath. Otherwise you will have a situation which gives no threat of trouble until the building is shaken by a nearby bomb and then down comes the ceiling with its load of sandbags, etc., and somebody is buried underneath.

Before shoring up make certain that the floor upon which the supports will stand is in itself strong enough to take the strain, and will not allow the timber to sink

21

PLATE 11

A CEILING LOOPHOLE

A hole has been made in the ceiling and butter-muslin has been stretched tightly over it. The man in the dark cockloft can see everything in the room below, but the loophole is not obvious.

The Boches are searching the house for a man they have seen, and the one on the right is just shouting "I'll bet the son of a pig-dog is in the wardrobe." As it happens, the pig-dog is only waiting for the third man to get into the room. Then he will fire three point-blank shots. Having done this he knows exactly what he will do, *i.e.*, run along the cockloft to the next house, steal downstairs to the cellar and pop up again in Plate 12, where he has prepared another surprise.

in should a heavy load be placed upon it by the sudden collapse of the house.

If there is in the unit a man from the building trade he will soon supervise the shoring up of a floor, but if not it is quite easy for unskilled men to make a thoroughly effective job if they see that the uprights are perfectly vertical and each one is wedged up to take its fair share of the work (Plate 17).

For shoring purposes it may be necessary to raid a blitzed house. The timber used should be the stoutest obtainable.

Do not forget that every cellar should have two exits, an extra one being easily made. Should there be any ground-floor windows which are weaknesses in the defence either from the enemy fire standpoint or liable to admit attackers, they should be blocked up entirely.

A good way to do this is to use double boarding or two sheets of corrugated iron with shingle (usually taken from the drive) in between. Shingle is first rate for stopping bullets, only a foot or so being required.

Having settled the downstairs windows turn your consideration to

THE ROOF

Can the enemy get on to the roof and attack downwards from there? Beware of this, because it is a most disconcerting thing to happen, as he will drop grenades down the chimney, snipe all round, and be most difficult to dislodge. If it is a flat roof it may be a grand place to put a couple of snipers; they may prevent the enemy from giving adequate covering fire and be able to exact a terrible toll during any attack on the house.

Some sandbags, grenades and Molotovs may be required on the roof, so do not overlook them.

Whilst considering the roof, see if visual communication can be established by flag or lamp with other parts of the town's defences, and if you can arrange a signal cord or speaking tube (hosepipe will do) to give alarm in house below by all means do so.

PLATE 12

LOOPHOLE IN THE FLOOR

Having popped up through a hole in the floor under the dining table the defender has seen two Boches in the room.

He has just, very sensibly, bumped off the one near the door first and is now scoring a dead centre on the other. After this he will not wait to see what happens, but he will go up the coal-chute (he has loosened the grating), along the entry and through two houses back to the Platoon Keep for tea.

Everything has been planned beforehand, including his get-away.

ENTRANCES

The various entrances to the house should be barricaded or, better still, protected by loopholed traverses, and if there are any narrow entries or passages they can be converted into traps by means of barbed wire and loopholes through which to fire or drop bombs.

Intercommunication between rooms, or houses if several are to be defended, should receive careful consideration.

Between houses joining up the cellars is usually the best way; particularly as it kills two birds with one stone by giving another exit.

It is very wise to have passages from room to room upstairs and down, and these may be concealed by wardrobes, cupboards, etc.

Sometimes good communication between two houses can be arranged right under the enemy's nose by judicious use of screens. He soon tires of firing promiscuously at the carpet or whatever it is you put up, and he cannot waste his ammunition because his future supplies are so problematic.

If you intend to have men upstairs do not forget to arrange bullet-proof cover against fire from downstairs.

Be sure to make adequate sanitary arrangements. Remember that high explosive is the world's finest laxative.

Should you have time, it will be worth your while to gas-proof a room, preferably the one you have strengthened.

Now let us attend to

PLATE 13

THE BAYONET LOOPHOLE

Useful for defence of passages and entries. The bottom of the loophole should be about three feet six inches from the ground.

The dotted soldier has just struck through the wall and hit the German in the kidneys. He will probably drop without a sound. The bayonet man then gets ready for the next invader, who is unlikely to have seen exactly how Fritz had been killed and consequently will advance past the loophole with his eyes glued to the front.

26

OUTSIDE THE HOUSE

Can we clear the field of fire? This requires doing with the greatest discrimination and, done cunningly, may be a decisive factor in the defence. Do not attempt to clear all round the house till it looks like a battleship cleared for action, but aim to make any cover there is a DEATH-TRAP TO THE ENEMY. I have mentioned using loopholes to induce them to attack some other side: dummy cover can be used even more effectively to persuade him to attack just where you want him to.

Usually round a house are various out-houses and garages which mask the defenders' fire and give an attacking enemy a covered approach. These should not be removed but should be so thinned out and opened up that the walls are not bullet-proof. During an attack in all probability the enemy will bunch behind them. Then a burst of fire can be sent *through* the building and they will trouble you no more. When preparing sheds, buildings, etc., in this way be sure you make the vulnerable area LOW DOWN; if you make it too high you may let one or two Huns still cling to life by lying down, whereas if you can shoot them through the legs the rest of them will drop into the vulnerable area.

It may be possible to coax the attacking enemy to take cover behind what looks like a large pile of debris but which is really canvas (or carpets) packed underneath with a few bricks and a little timber thrown on for effect. The pile looks as if it would stop an A/T bullet, but actually a tommy-gun can shoot right through it.

Barbed wire can be of great help, particularly during darkness or in smoke or fog. It should not be placed where it can be seen by the enemy from either the ground or the air. Coiled in entries, alleys, passageways, etc., it can be a great obstacle to the enemy.

All wire should have tins, etc., hung on it to give the alarm if anyone shakes it, and it MUST BE COVERED BY FIRE.

The latter requirement is met if grenades can be

PLATE 14

HOW TO SHOOT A GERMAN UP THROUGH THE GRATING

After waiting amongst the coal the Home Guard heard the German tip-toeing along the street. When he was over the grating the Home Guard let him have it! A shot-gun is all right for this close work, but if you want to knock their helmets off you must use a rifle.

exploded in the wire. You realize, of course, that if the wire is not covered in some way the enemy may remove it and attack you unexpectedly.

Whilst considering the outside of the house, see if there is any place from which the enemy could dominate the buildings you are going to hold. If there is, you will have to do something about it—either occupy the place yourself or put men where they can by accurate rifle fire prevent the enemy from occupying the threatening point.

For instance, you may find that the enemy could, if they occupied the roof of the house across the road, make it very hot for you, but if you put men on the roof of *your* house no one could live on the roof across the road.

After settling this, have a look round for DEAD GROUND and if you find some within hitting distance see what can be done by way of making fresh rifle positions, etc., to bring it under fire.

Failing this, you will have to consider a detached post to look after it or putting wire or other obstacles to prevent the enemy using it.

The next outside matter to attend to is to decide which is the best approach for your own men by day and by night. If the state of emergency lasts a long time you will require rations, reliefs, etc., bringing up and these should come unobtrusively or they may give away the position to the enemy.

Which reminds me to emphasize that nothing you do to the house or its surroundings should give the least indication to the enemy that it is to be defended.

If you decide to take the glass out of some of the windows take some out of the surrounding houses as well. If you put some dummy heaps of rubble in the garden, as I have just suggested, put some REAL heaps in the neighbouring gardens.

It may be advisable to dig a few slit trenches for the protection of your men in air raids, bombardment, etc. If you cannot entirely hide these, dig some in other

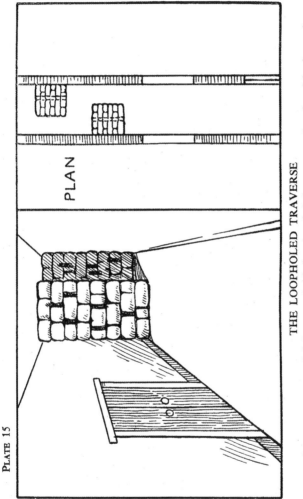

PLATE 15

PLAN

THE LOOPHOLED TRAVERSE

Here is a passage guarded by men behind a loopholed traverse. On the right is a plan. Two men can fire along the corridor and they are difficult to rush, particularly if the passage is filled with dannert wire.

To disguise the actual loopholes dummy openings have been painted or made in various parts of the traverse.

gardens near by. Should it be impossible to avoid making tracks in the garden which may show up from the air be sure to make similar tracks in the gardens all round.

Sometimes it is a good idea to make some other house look as if it has been put in a state of defence, particularly if you can enfilade the enemy who may be induced to attack it.

And in your study of the surroundings *never forget* that ATTACK IS THE BEST DEFENCE, so be prepared with schemes for counter-attacking the enemy should he be held up near to your house.

Next give the place the " once-over " from the standpoint of FIRE. Should there be a lot of inflammable refuse, etc., inside the house have it removed to a safe distance. Commandeer all the fire-fighting equipment you can get hold of and put it at suitable points. Keep your eye on the supplies of water and sand. Turn off the electricity and gas supplies at the meter.

When your preparations are complete, look everywhere for signs of activity which will tell the enemy the house is defended. Trails of white plaster into the garden—piles of painfully new rubbish—altered windows—sandbags showing—loopholes obvious—dust out in the road, etc.—are all indications which may cause enemy scouts, aerial or ground, to suspect your house.

Now, having discussed the material side of the defence, let us talk about

PLATE 16

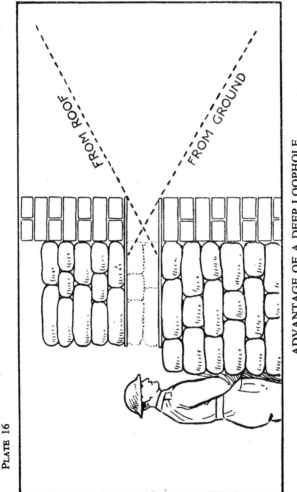

ADVANTAGE OF A DEEP LOOPHOLE

This loophole has been sited to cover one particular spot. Should an enemy sniper get on the roof opposite he is too high up to shoot straight into the loophole, and if he goes to ground level he is too low.

Sandbags should be arranged as shown to catch the bullets, otherwise they may ricochet into the face of the look-out.

THE MEN

How many do we need? How will they act? Where will they be kept?

Before we start answering these queries let us be absolutely sure you have the right idea about what the men will do.

Dismiss for ever any lingering Maginot complex which may be inclining you to look on the defended house as a place in which to await the enemy.

All this " awaiting the enemy " idea is so much bunk! So long as we are content to wait for the enemy to start doing things to us we shall continue to get the worst of it.

No! The defended house should be the centre for defensive activity taking place in the surrounding district. It is a wasp's nest from which the wasps will dart out and STING!

Possibly after heavy fighting the house MAY be the scene of a last desperate stand against the invader, but till that time comes it should be regarded only as a base for operations and there must be no tendency to keep within its precincts when there is an enemy who can be ATTACKED.

Generally speaking, to defend a house requires only a few men—say, six, eight or ten—and these may possibly be detailed to act as garrison cooks, etc., while the house itself is used for feeding and rest by fighting patrols and similar bodies of men who will come and go.

We are concerned now only with the garrison, as fighting patrol, street fighting and tank-hunting parties have been dealt with elsewhere. The garrison should be organized in pairs, and every man should know his job. A look-out must always be kept to obviate risk of surprise attack, and all men should be warned against hanging about anywhere in view of aircraft or enemy scouts.

Even with such a small garrison it is very advisable

PLATE 17

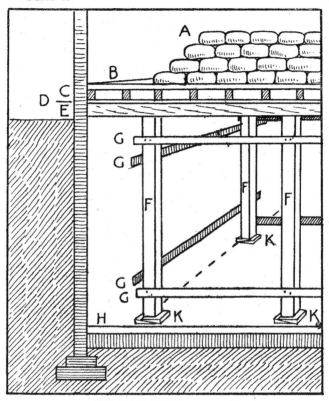

SHORING UP A CEILING

A.—Sandbags.
B.—Floor.
C.—Joists.
D.—Ceiling.
E.—Top plate (stout planks).
F.—Uprights.
G.—Braces.
H.—Sole plate (in case floor is weak).
K.—Wedges (two under each upright).

The wedges are used to adjust the uprights so that each one takes its share of the weight. If the bottom braces get in the way leave them out. Shoring is done when a considerable weight is to be put on to the floor above or to give safety in case house collapses through bombing.

always to have a reserve (if only two men) in some central place ready to rally round instantly and stage a counter-attack should the enemy unexpectedly penetrate the defences.

If the garrison has an automatic weapon, such as an L.M.G. or tommy-gun, it will usually be wiser to put it where there is a POOR field of fire. That is where the enemy is likely to rush across. If you put the weapon where there is the best field of fire it will probably never get a target, because that is just where the Germans will NOT come.

See that all your bombs are detonated and suitably distributed for use, and if you have some A/T mines make detailed plans as to how they will be used and who will use them. You will be able to form a fairly reliable idea of how tanks will approach the house.

Consider the question of posting one or two snipers in the surrounding district, with careful instructions about their withdrawal.

If you have time, go and liaise with the other defended houses in the vicinity.

It will give you a good idea of correct tactics in defending a house if I describe what took place at

PLATE 18

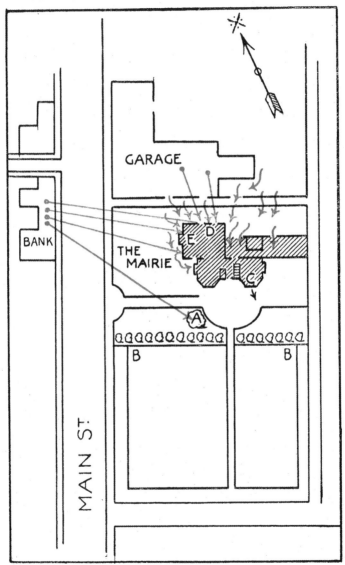

THE FIGHT AT THE MAIRIE

THE MAIRIE (Plate 18)

This was a large, strongly built house standing well back from the main street. To the north of it was a large garage and across the street the bank.

As the enemy was reported to be approaching rapidly from the south, Lieut. T was ordered by his company commander to place the Mairie in a state of defence and hold it, with the remains of his platoon, whatever might happen.

T, who was a very conscientious officer, at once posted a man at an upstairs window with orders to keep a keen look-out in the enemy's direction, and ordered his L.M.G. team to dig in at A under the shade of a large tree, so as to cover the garden, which offered an excellent field of fire. He had a small quantity of barbed wire and this he used to strengthen the hedge at B, making it into a very formidable obstacle.

His stores and S.A.A., together with several wounded men, he put into the cellar, gas-proofing the door with blankets.

Knowing the enemy to be in close proximity, he periodically called upstairs " Are you keeping a good look-out across the garden? " and he always received a reassuring " Yessir! " from above.

As he was expecting the enemy from the south and there was such a good field of fire in that direction, he stationed his tommy-gun at C, well back in the dining-room, ready to fire through the open window.

To give all-round defence he placed men in the rooms at D and E, both upstairs and downstairs.

These men were waiting for some sandbags to arrive from Company Headquarters so that they could start making some protection for themselves, when suddenly there was a terrific racket from the roofs of the garage and the bank.

This was covering fire for a number of Germans who swarmed out of the garage and were crossing the entry as the men at D and E reached the windows. Before they could fire at the attacking enemy they were shot down by the accurate covering fire from the roofs opposite, which smashed through the windows with deadly precision.

A few seconds later the Boches were in the house shooting the tommy-gun and L.M.G. teams in the back before they could fire a shot. The upstairs look-out came to the top of the stairs and was immediately scuppered by bullets from below.

A hand grenade thrown into the cellar completed the wiping out of the garrison. This the Germans had done *without sustaining a casualty.*

If, as is said to happen, Lieut. T in the short time he lived after receiving three bayonet wounds could have reviewed the events leading to his death he would have realized what fundamental blunders he had made: —

1. He had assumed that because the enemy were approaching from the south they would ATTACK from that direction. His continual calling to the look-out man had served only to rivet his attention on the GARDEN while the enemy was sneaking up the back alleys and side streets. If he had only sent out a couple of scouts to contact the enemy he would have been warned in time.

2. He had placed his automatic weapons, his all-important fire power, where he HOPED the enemy would come, and not where common sense would have told him they were much more likely to come. The Germans are seldom obliging enough to attack over a good field of fire if there is a covered approach from some other direction.

3. He had not occupied the Mairie roof. If he had placed a couple of good shots there the Germans could never have given covering fire from the roofs of either the garage or the bank, and his own men at D and E could have shot down the advancing Germans like rabbits.

4. He had placed the precious barbed wire in the very place the enemy would be most unlikely to reach it, whereas if he had put it between the garage and the house it would have held them up under heavy fire, which is the special function of barbed wire.

5. He had not barricaded the doors and windows and so they had been easily rushed.

6. He had not put a barricade or a loopholed traverse to prevent the enemy mounting the stairs.

7. He had allowed his men to waste time waiting for sandbags when they could have been using the material on the spot, filling drawers with gravel from the drive, or soil out of the garden; barricading doors and passages with furniture, mattresses and so on.

8. He had not kept an organized reserve. Even a few men in some place where they could not be taken by surprise and all ready to counter-attack instantly would have held up the enemy long enough for the tommy-gun and the L.M.G. to come into action, and this might have saved the situation.

Poor T! He learnt a lot in the last few seconds of his life, but it was too late then for him to benefit.

But it is not too late for us to benefit. The lesson is that it is no use waiting for the Royal Engineers to put our house in order. It is for US to do it, with every ounce of energy and common sense we possess. No use lamenting because we have no dump of material to draw upon: we must use the timber, wire, furniture, carpets and anything else which is to hand on the spot.

And, just as a last word upon this subject of the defence of houses, I would impress upon you once again LET YOUR DEFENCE BE ACTIVE; GO OUT AND HIT THE ENEMY FIRST; KEEP HITTING HIM AS HE DRAWS NEAR TO YOUR DEFENDED HOUSE; and have your defences so good and so cunning, both inside and outside, that when he begins to attack it you can heave a sigh of relief and say, " And now he's going to ask for it and he *will* GET IT! "

First published by Gale & Polden, *c*.1942

This edition published by Royal Armouries Museum,
Armouries Drive, Leeds LS10 1LT, United Kingdom
www.royalarmouries.org

ISBN 978 1 91301 302 8

A CIP record for this book is available from the British Library

Every effort has been made to contact copyright holders.
Royal Armouries will be happy to correct any errors or omissions
brought to their attention.

Typesetting by Typo•glyphix

10 9 8 7 6 5 4 3 2 1

The original version of Defence of Houses contained
black and red diagrams, which have been reproduced here in greyscale.
Mention of colour in the text has been retained for accuracy.